"Round the Beading Twist"

Creative Cordmaking

by
Jacqui Carey

"OTT" Embellishment series - Book Two.
Ideal for any textile enthusiast who wishes to
create complimentary embellishments.
Exploring simple yet effective techniques that
require little or no equipment.
"Round the Beading Twist" looks at new ideas
for the simple twisted cord
and how to combine it with beads.

*Colour reproduction, design and photography by
Carey Company.
Printed by Elkar mccgraphics.
Published by Carey Company.*

ISBN: 0 9523225 5 2

Round the Beading Twist

In order to avoid repetition and to dedicate more space to new ideas, it has been assumed that readers are familiar with book one "Round the Twist'. This second book looks at how techniques described in book one can be combined with beads to create stunning new cords. It also includes a few more methods that can be used with, or without beads.

You can use any type of bead and you can incorporate them with all sorts of cords (materials are illustrated on page 26 & 27). The samples in this book will give you a few ideas to get you started, but there are many, many more waiting to be discovered.

Twisted cords make ideal trimmings for fashion and furnishings, especially when they are tailor-made for the project. There are numerous other uses including cords for glasses, bag handles and jewellery. The beaded cords are particularly well suited for making into jewellery and can even be especially colour co-ordinated for particular outfits!

Sample 8 (see page 9) being used as a sumptuous curtain tieback.

Basic Threading

Threading beads onto a twisted cord is an obvious way of combining the two. Beads with large holes usually give the best results, but try to avoid ones with rough or chipped holes. These can damage the threads and can even cause the cord to break. Another tip is to run some spare thread or a pipe cleaner through the hole to check that it is clean and free from residue.

The size of the hole in a bead can vary. You will even find a few tapered holes, with one end a different diameter to the other. Before starting to make a cord for a particular project, it is worth making a short sample to check that the cord will fit. Adding or subtracting a few threads can achieve exactly the right diameter. Don't forget that the action of 'twisting' will increase the diameter and that 'folding' will automatically double the quantity of your original bundle of threads.

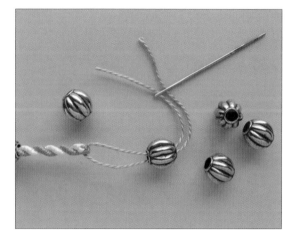

If the cord is sufficiently snug inside the hole, it will prevent the bead from slipping along the cord. This means that you can space several beads along a necklace without them all sliding together.

It is best to pull, rather than push, the cord through the beads especially if it is a snug fit. The 'looped end' (page 23 in book one) is ideal for this. Slip a single thread through the 'looped end' and take both ends of the thread through the eye of a needle. You can now use the needle and thread to pull the cord through beads.

Sample 1 (with different colour variations).
Make a cord from 8 strands of cream Perle joined 'end-to-end' with 8 strands of ochre Perle and twisted in a clockwise direction. Thread melon beads onto the finished cord.

Multiple Threading

Attractive results can be obtained by threading several cords through one bead. It does make a difference which direction you thread the cords through the bead. Cords can enter the bead hole from the same side or from opposite directions.

If cords are always taken through from the same side they will run parallel to each other (see Sample 2), but if cords always enter the hole from opposite directions, a more circular effect is created (see Sample 3). And of course, you can always alternate between the two (see Sample 4). In fact any combination of threading can be used in one project. The necklace on the opposite page uses basic threading for the smaller beads and multiple threading for the larger ones.

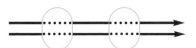

Two cords threaded through the beads from the same side

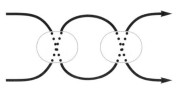

Two cords threaded through the beads from opposite directions.

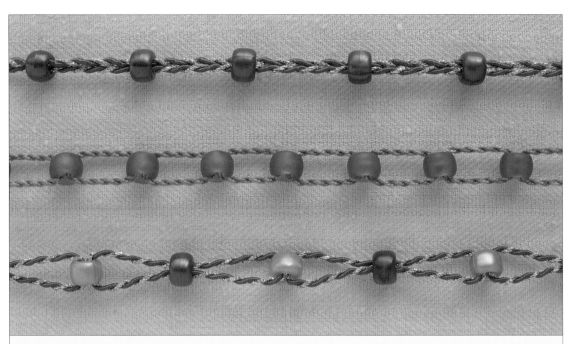

Sample 2 (top).
Make a cord from 1 strand of mauve Gimp joined 'end-to-end' with 2 strands of silver Glitter and twisted in a clockwise direction. Make another cord using the same threads but twisted in an anti-clockwise direction. Thread both cords through purple Pony beads, entering the bead hole from the same side.
Sample 3 (centre).
Make two cords, each from 2 strands of variegated Perle twisted in a clockwise direction. Thread the cords through mauve Pony beads, with the cords entering the bead hole from opposite directions.
Sample 4 (bottom).
Make two cords, each from 1 strand of mauve Gimp joined 'end-to-end' with 2 strands of silver Glitter and twisted in an anti-clockwise direction. Thread both cords through purple and mauve Pony beads, entering the bead hole alternately from the opposite, then same direction.

Multiple Threading

A necklace made from ten different cords (details on page 20 & 21) and a selection of silver beads. The cords always remain parallel, with several cords entering the ring beads from the same direction. Different cords go through each ring bead.

Wrapping - Plain Strings

Wrapping (page 12 in book one) a string of beads around a finished cord is an ideal way of jazzing up your work. It is possible to buy ready-made strings but you can easily make your own. To get a rough idea of how long a string you will need, temporarily wrap a spare thread around the cord and mark the required length. Remove the spare thread and use it as a measure for the string of beads. You will need a fine but strong thread and a suitable needle (see page 27). The thread will need to be approximately 20cm (8 inches) longer than the measure to allow for the stitching at each end.

Plain Strings - Method.

1. Add the first bead and make a half hitch over it so that it sits approximately 10cm (4 inches) from the end.

Half hitch over bead

2. Continue to make the string by taking the needle through the required length of beads.

3. Make sure that the beads are pushed up along the string, against the first bead. Then use the end of the thread to stitch the string into the start of the cord.

4. Wrap the string of beads around the cord.

5. Undo the half hitch before stitching the other end of the thread into the cord.

Beads are heavy and have no elasticity, so they can end up drooping away from the cord. To prevent this, make sure the string is wrapped snugly into the groove. You may have to add or subtract a few beads to get the correct length.

Sample 5 (detail).
Make a cord from 6 strands of ochre Gimp twisted in a clockwise direction. Make another cord from 20 strands of black Perle joined 'end-to-end' with 20 strands of cream Perle and twisted in a clockwise direction. Join the two cords together and re-twist them anti-clockwise. Wrap an ochre Gimp into one groove and a string of tiger's eye chips into the other.

Wrapping - Plain Strings

Sample 6.
Make a cord from 8 strands of cream Gimp joined 'end-to-end' with 12 strands of cream Glitter and twisted in a clockwise direction. Join the cord 'end-to-end' with 40 strands of cream Perle and re-twist in an anti-clockwise direction. Wrap a string of pearl size 11/0 rocaille beads into both grooves.

A necklace made from Sample 5 and finished with brass bellcaps and a clasp (see page 22).

Wrapping - Fancy Strings

An alternative to taking the needle and thread regularly through each bead is to connect beads together using a variety of stitches. The idea dates back to the ancient Egyptians and is known as 'off-loom beadwork'. The technique has been used in many ways to create different types of work, but it is not usually combined with other techniques such as cordmaking.

Although the 'Spiral Fan' and 'Double Fan' work well by themselves, they are more dramatic when combined with the cords. The 'Spiral Fan' is designed to curve naturally around the groove of a cord, whilst the 'Double Fan' allows a cord to be wrapped around the beadwork.

These flowers, made by Lynn Firth, show just one of the many styles of 'off-loom beadwork'.

'Spiral Fan' - Method.
Start.
Thread the needle through the following beads: bugle,
size 11/0 rocaille,
size 6/0 rocaille,
size 11/0 rocaille,
bugle.
Knot the ends of the thread together and take the needle back through the first bugle.

Working Sequence.
1. Add a size 11/0 rocaille, size 6/0 rocaille, size 11/0 rocaille, bugle.
2. Take the needle back through the bugle, three rocaille beads and bugle.
3. Add a bugle, size 11/0 rocaille, size 6/0 rocaille and a size 11/0 rocaille.
4. Take the needle back through two bugles.

Repeat Steps 1 to 4 until the desired length is achieved.

'Double Fan' - Method.
Start.
As 'Spiral Fan'.

Working Sequence.
As 'Spiral Fan' except work repeats of Steps 1, 2, 3, 4, 3, and 4.

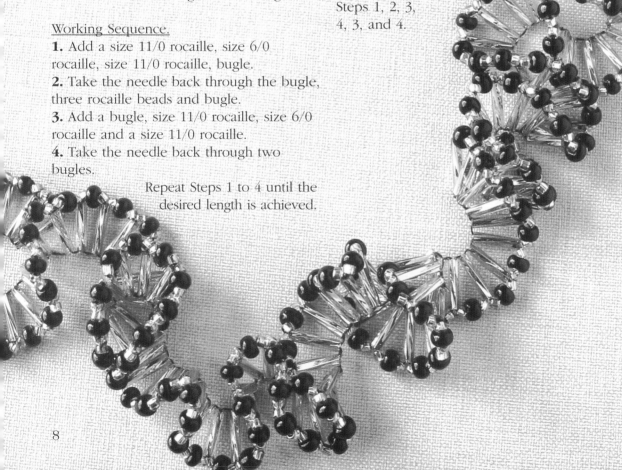

Wrapping - Fancy Strings

Diagrams for working sequence.

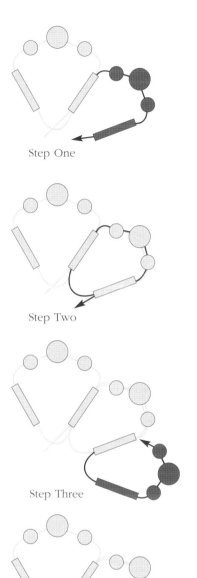

Step One

Step Two

Step Three

Step Four

Sample 7 (left).
Make a length of 'Double Fan' using gold twisted bugles, gold iridescent size 11/0 and black size 6/0 rocailles. Make a cord from 2 strands of turquoise Gimp joined 'end-to-end' with 2 strands of blue Gimp and twisted in a clockwise direction. Wrap the cord around the 'Double Fan' beadwork.
Sample 8 (right).
Make a length of 'Spiral Fan'. Make a cord using the instructions for Sample 5 (see page 5) but instead of using a string of tiger's eye chips, wrap the cord with the 'Spiral Fan' beadwork.

Beading the Threads

Amore integrated way of combining beads and cords is to put the beads onto the thread before the cord is made. You can add the odd one or two to give a 'dew drop' effect (see Sample 9) or you can cover the thread entirely, so that you are twisting strings of beads (see Sample 10). Whatever you do, you will need a thread that is fine enough to go through the beads and strong enough to take the strain of twisting. One way of getting more thread through a bead is to use a leading thread, so that the bead goes over the eye of the needle and the bulk of the thread separately. Alternatively, the beads can sit on a finer thread that runs parallel to the main thread of the cord (see Sample 9).

The leading thread goes between the threads for the cord and into the eye of the beading needle

Special consideration needs to be given when working with a single string of beads (such as Sample 11). This is because the beads will remain static whilst the thread inside does all of the twisting. You will need to prepare your string using a strong thread that sits loosely inside the bead hole and is longer than the total length of beads. For example, 70cm (27inches) of beads spread over 1 metre (39inches) of thread will allow for the 'take-up' and still give you plenty of room for your fingers to twist the thread.

Sample 9.
Put a few blue size 11/0 rocailles on 1 strand of thick beading thread. Lay 4 of these prepared threads parallel to 16 strands of navy Perle (see photo detail). Make a cord from the 4 beaded threads and 16 strands of Perle joined 'end-to-end' with 6 strands of blue Gimp and twisted in a clockwise direction.

Beading the Threads

Sample 10.
Make a cord from 4 strings of iridescent blue size 11/0 rocailles joined 'end-to-end' with 4 strings of frosted blue size 11/0 rocailles and twisted in a clockwise direction.

Sample 11.
Make a cord from 1 string of iridescent blue size 11/0 rocailles joined 'end-to-end' with 1 string of iridescent yellow size 11/0 rocailles and twisted in a clockwise direction.

Sample 12.
Make a cord from 1 string of mottled blue Double Delica beads joined 'end-to-end' with 6 strands of yellow Perle and twisted in a clockwise direction.

Sample 13.
Make a cord from 1 string of yellow size 8/0 rocailles twisted in a clockwise direction. Make another cord from 4 strands of navy Gimp twisted in a clockwise direction. Join the two cords 'end-to-end' and re-twist in an anti-clockwise direction. Wrap a Fancy Ribbon One into one of the grooves.

Sample 14.
Make a cord from 1 string of blue size 6/0 rocailles joined 'end-to-end' with 16 strands of navy Perle and twisted in a clockwise direction. Join this cord 'end-to-end' with 4 strands of blue Gimp and re-twist in an anti-clockwise direction.

Distorting

Interesting effects can be created by distorting a cord, so that one helix is shorter than the other. Unfortunately, it is not an easy process to control when using the 'twist and fold' method and the results can end up rather wild (see Sample 15a). It is possible to start with two different lengths joined 'end-to-end', so that when they have been twisted and folded, the take-up of one helix is different to the other. However, you may find it easier to start with each helix the same length, then distort the cord after it is finished. This is done by pulling hard on one helix. The down side of this method is that some of the thread is wasted.

Distorting - Method.

1. Twist and fold a cord in the usual way, but instead of securing the end, pinch it between the thumb and forefinger of the left hand.
2. With the right hand, pull hard on the threads that you want to be the shorter, internal helix. Allow the threads to slide through your left-hand fingers without losing any of the twist.

Three different effects created by distorting the same cord.
Sample 15a (Left): The longer helix twists back on itself to form little branches protruding from the main cord.
Sample 15b (Centre): The longer helix circles neatly over the other helix.
Sample 15c (Right): The longer helix completely covers the other helix.

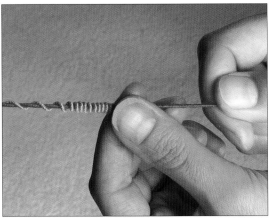

You may need to tweak the threads as you go. Sometimes it helps to over distort the cord so that it looks like Sample 15c before easing the helix back to look like Sample 15b.
3. Secure the cord and remove the waste thread.

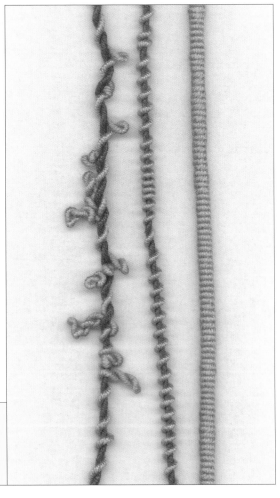

Sample 15a, b & c.
Make a cord from 4 strands of dark pink Perle joined 'end-to-end' with 4 strands of pale pink Perle and twisted in a clockwise direction. Distort by pulling on the dark pink helix.

Distorting

You can try distorting other types of cord, such as re-twisted ones (see Sample 32, page 21) and beaded ones like the one on this page. It has been made into a necklace with a central bead. Eyepin Links are a useful way of attaching large beads with small holes.

Making Eyepin Links.

Thread the bead on to a metal eyepin.

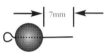

Trim the metal to approximately 7mm (¼ inch) from the end of the bead.

Use round nose pliers to form a second eye.

Sample 16.
Put some mauve size 8/0 rocailles onto 2 strands of mauve Perle. Join this 'end-to-end' with 4 strands of green Viscose and twist in an anti-clockwise direction. Distort the cord by pulling on the green helix.
The lampwork bead has been attached by inserting an Eyepin Link through the bead and into the Looped Ends (page 23 in book one).

Samples

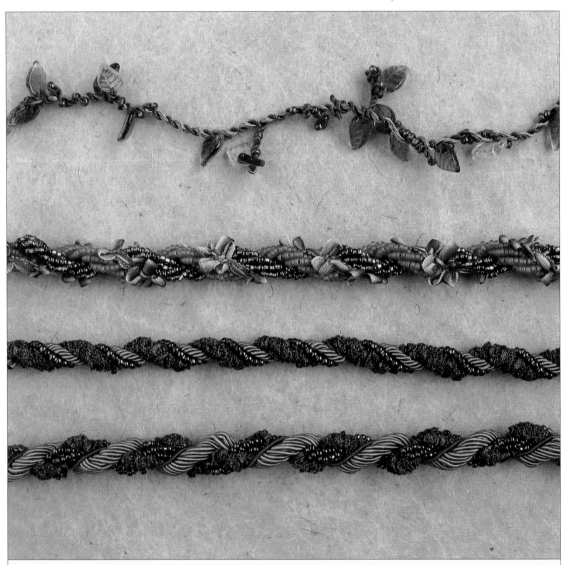

From top to bottom:

Sample 17.

Prepare a random selection of mauve size 8/0 rocailles and leaf beads onto 2 strands of olive Perle. Make a cord from these 2 strands joined 'end-to-end' with 4 strands of green Viscose and twisted in a clockwise direction. Distort the cord by pulling on the Viscose.

Sample 18.

Make a cord from 4 strings of iridescent green size 11/0 rocailles joined 'end-to-end' with 4 strings of frosted green size 11/0 rocailles and twisted in a clockwise direction. Wrap a Fancy Ribbon Two into one of the grooves.

Sample 19.

Make a cord from 4 strands of green Gimp joined 'end-to-end' with 1 strand of green Ruched Ribbon and twisted in a clockwise direction. Wrap a string of iridescent red size 8/0 rocailles into one of the grooves.

Sample 20.

Make a cord from 3 strings of iridescent red size 11/0 rocailles joined 'end-to-end' with 1 strand of green Ruched Ribbon and twisted in a clockwise direction. Join this cord 'end-to-end' with 16 strands of light green Gimp and re-twist in an anti-clockwise direction. Wrap a dark green Gimp into one of the grooves.

Opposite: Sample 20 with beaded tassel ends (see page 24).

Ply-splitting

Cords are held together by a twisting force. If you open up the space between each helix of a cord, you will notice that they try to squeeze themselves back together. The tighter your cords, the stronger the force. This can be used to hold all sorts of things between the plies of a cord. It can even be strong enough to use as a pegless washing line!

Some interesting effects can be created by taking something through the plies of a cord, a process known as ply-splitting.

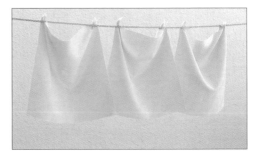

Method for ply-splitting a single cord.

1. Make a cord in the usual way.

2. At the start of the cord, open up a space between the plies and pass an item through it (Sample 21 uses a string of beads)

3. Let the space close, then open up another space below it, ready to receive the next passing.

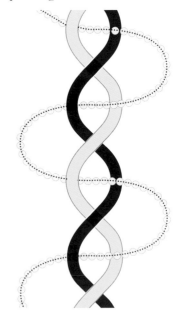

Sample 21.
Make a cord from 20 strands of navy Perle joined 'end-to-end' with 20 strands of gold Glitter and twisted in a clockwise direction. Ply-split with a string of mauve size 10/0 rocailles, zigzagging them back and forth through the cord with just one twist of the cord between each split (as shown in the diagram).

Ply-splitting

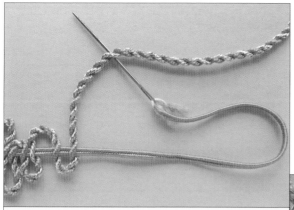

It is not necessary to use equipment, but it can be helpful. Needles, crochet hooks, forceps, latchet hooks and other specialist tools can all be used to help draw items through the cord.

Sample 22 (above).
Make a cord from 4 strands of ochre Perle joined 'end-to-end' with 4 strands of yellow Glitter thread and twisted in a clockwise direction. Pass a Russia braid between the plies of the cord, zigzagging back and forth but vary the distance (and number of twists in the cord) between each split. Pull the Russia braid so that it is the cord that curves whilst the Russia braid remains straight.
Choker (below).
This is made using Sample 22. The cord is measured so that at the halfway point, both the cord and the Russia braid are taken through the hole in a 'Jazzy Lily' lampwork bead (see detail above). Work then continues to complete the ply-splitting. Both ends of the Russia braid are left unworked, so that they can be used to tie the choker.

Ply-splitting

Ply-splitting with more than one cord.

We have seen that a certain amount of variation can be gained from working with a single cord, but the potential increases when working with two, or more cords. When working with a pair of cords, there are two ways in which they can be connected together: by opening up the space between the plies on either cord.

These two types of connections can be used in various combinations. The possibilities are endless and have been used to produce a range of traditional designs.

Traditional work tends to be made with plain cords, but there is no reason why you cannot work with the fancy cords, including beaded ones. Just a few cords will produce some wonderful textured results !

The left-hand, mauve cord can go through the space in the right-hand, ochre cord or vice versa.

Extract from the book 'The Techniques of Ply-Split Braiding' by Peter Collingwood. It shows a detail of a traditional camel girth, made from many cords ply-split together.

Sample 23.
Make 5 identical cords, each from 1 string of gold lined, size 11/0 rocailles joined 'end-to-end' with 1 string of iridescent orange, size 8/0 rocailles and twisted in an anti-clockwise direction. Make another cord from 1 strand of ochre Gimp twisted in an anti-clockwise direction. Join the cords together so that the Gimp cord starts on the left-hand side and ply-split them together using the method shown on opposite page. (A neat start has been made by taking the Gimp cord between the plies at the beginning of each bead cord. It is then taken back through the 'loop end' of the Gimp cord)

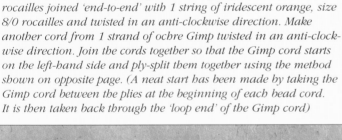

Ply-splitting

Method.

1. Make several cords and join them together in the correct order.

2. Starting from the left and working towards the right, take the left most (in Sample 23, this is the Gimp) cord between the plies of each cord in turn, until it reaches the right-hand side.

3. Now work from right to left, taking the right most (in Sample 23, this is the Gimp) cord between the plies of each cord in turn, until it is back on the left-hand side.

4. Continue working back and forth, leaving one twist between the openings in the cords.

Sample 24.
Make a cord from 4 strands of mauve Knitting Ribbon twisted in an anti-clockwise direction. Join this cord 'end-to-end' with 6 strands of purple Gimp and re-twist in a clockwise direction. Make another indentical cord. Make 2 other cords, each from 8 strands of ochre Perle twisted in a clockwise direction. Join the cords together so that they sit alternately: fancy, Perle, fancy, Perle.
Plysplit them together using the method shown, except omit step 3. This means that for each 'row', a different cord is taken through the other three. (Photo detail shows the fancy cord has just been taken through the other three. Now the Perle is on the left-hand side, ready to make the next 'row'). Allow two twists in the cord that is passing through the three others and the usual one twist in all other places.
Diana East's pendant lampwork bead has been stitched in place after the ply-splitting.

Ends & Joins

It is the finishing touches that can turn a sample into a beautiful product. Some ideas of how to finish off beaded twisted cords have already been discussed (such as ties on page 17 and the neat start on page 18). There are many other possibilities that can be explored. You can permanently join cords together to make a necklace or bracelet, or you can use a clasp. There are many different types available so you can choose your favourite type. Alternatively, you can finish the ends of a cord to form a feature point, such as the beaded tassels on page 24.

Complete Join.

You can join together the two ends of a cord to form a continuous circle. The join can then be hidden with a decorative feature such as beadwork or a fancy whipping. Using this method, you can also connect several cords together.

Joining - Method.

1. Make a permanent whipping over both the start and the finish of the cord. Trim away the loose threads. (If you are joining several cords together, you may wish to make small permanent whippings over every end before making a larger one to connect all the cords together.)

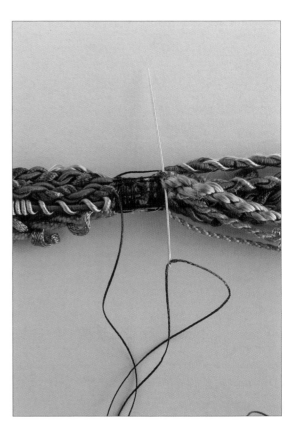

3. Hide the join with beadwork or whip a matching cord over the top (as seen in this example where a piece of Sample 26 has been used). Tuck both ends of this cord into the whipping and stitch them in place with a matching thread.

2. Bring both ends together so that the whippings butt up against each other. Then stitch across the whippings. The first few stitches are tricky to hold but it gets easier as you work around the circumference.

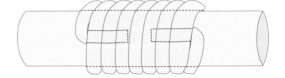

Ends & Joins

Detail showing Samples 25 to 34 joined together to form the necklace shown on page 5.

From top to bottom:
Sample 25.
Make a cord from a single strand of variegated mauve Perle twisted in a clockwise direction.
Sample 26.
Make a cord from 2 strands of variegated mauve Floss twisted in a clockwise direction.
Sample 27.
Make a cord from 2 strands of variegated mauve Floss twisted in an anti-clockwise direction.
Sample 28.
Make a cord from 2 strands of variegated mauve Perle joined 'parallel' with a single beading thread (threaded with a scattering of silver lined size 11/0 rocailles) and twisted in an anti-clockwise direction.
Sample 29.
Make a cord from 2 strands of mauve Gimp joined 'end-to-end' with 2 strands of variegated mauve Perle (threaded with a scattering of silver lined size 11/0 rocailles) and twisted in a clockwise direction.
Sample 30.
Make a cord from 2 strands of variegated mauve Floss joined 'end-to-end' with 1 strand of variegated Knitting Ribbon and twisted in an anti-clockwise direction.
Sample 31.
Make a cord from 2 strands of mauve Gimp joined 'end-to-end' with 2 strands of variegated Knitting Ribbon and twisted in an anti-clockwise direction.
Sample 32.
Make a cord from 1 strand of variegated Knitting Ribbon twisted in a clockwise direction. Join this cord 'end-to-end' with 2 strands of mauve Gimp and re-twist in an anti-clockwise direction.
Distort the cord by pulling on the Gimp.
Sample 33.
Make a cord from 1 strand of mauve Gimp joined 'end-to-end' with 1 strand of variegated Floss and twisted in a clockwise direction. Distort the cord by pulling on the Gimp.
Sample 34.
Make a cord from 2 strands of variegated mauve Perle twisted in a clockwise direction. Ply-split a strand of Knitting Ribbon randomly back and forth through the plies.

Ends & Joins

Clasps.

Most clasps can be stitched onto the end of a cord, either directly into the threads or, as in the necklace opposite, into the beadwork. It is worth making several stitches through the clasp so that it is strong enough to take the strain.

Alternatively, the clasps can be attached to bellcaps, which provide a neat finish to a cord.

Bellcaps - Method.

1. Make a small permanent whipping on the ends of the cord and trim away the loose threads.

2. Make sure that the bellcap is the correct fit before applying a small amount of 2-part epoxy adhesive (such as Araldite) onto the ends of the cord.
3. Push the bellcap into place and leave to dry.

Detail of the necklace on page 7. The clasp is attached to 7mm brass bellcaps.

Bugle Ferrule - Method.

<u>Start</u>
Take a needle and thread through 2 bugles and knot the thread together. Then take the needle and thread back through one of the bugles.

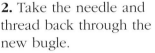

<u>Working Sequence</u>
1. Add a new bugle and take the needle and thread back through the old bugle.
2. Take the needle and thread back through the new bugle.
Continue repeating steps 1 and 2 until you have enough length to fit around the cord.

<u>Finish</u>
Roll the bugles around the cord so that the last bugle meets the first bugle. Take the needle and thread through the first bugle and back through the last bugle. Tighten the work and stitch along the edges of the beadwork into the cord to secure it in place.

Work in progress finishing the ends of the necklace on opposite page.

Ends & Joins

A necklace made using a blue version of Sample 8. The 'Spiral Fan' has a clasp added in place of a size 6/0 rocaille in the last fan. The end of the cord has been finished with a permanent whipping and the loose threads removed. The whipping is covered with a Bugle Ferrule (see opposite page). To finish the ends, the 'Spiral Fan' has been wrapped over ferrule and stitched down into a swirl inside the ferrule (see photo detail right).

Ends & Joins

Beadwork Tassels.

Tasselmaking is a whole new book full of ideas, but a straightforward beadwork skirt is sufficient to give a simple but effective embellishment over the thread tassel. Plenty of variation can be found by trying different combinations of bead types and lengths.

Beadwork skirt - Method.

1. Make a permanent whipping on the cord and trim the threads into a neat tassel.

2. Secure some beading thread into the cord just above the whipping.

3. The first 'column' of the skirt is made by adding the required length of beads and one last bead (the first skirt in Sample 35 has twenty-five rocailles and the last bead is a dagger).

4. Miss the last (dagger) bead and take the needle and thread back up through all of the other beads.

5. Take the needle and thread back into the cord and out where you want the next column of beads to start.

6. Continue working around the circumference of the cord until sufficient columns of beads have been added.

Sample 20 (on page 15) has tassels made using a version of the beadwork skirt. The cord has been whipped and the loose threads removed. The whipping has then been covered with a Bugle Ferrule (see page 22). A green Ruched Ribbon has been whipped over the cord to add volume (see photo above). The beadwork skirt is then stitched into the cord, between the bugles and Ruched Ribbon. The beadwork skirt is made from a random selection of green beads: mixed shades and sizes of rocailles, bugles and 4mm faceted beads. To finish the piece, a few beads have been stitched onto the Ruched Ribbon.

Ends & Joins

Sample 35.
 Make a cord from 30 strands of ochre Perle joined
'end-to-end' with 30 strands of yellow Glitter and
twisted in an anti-clockwise direction. Wrap a
string of iridescent orange, size 8/0 rocailles in one
groove. The first beadwork skirt is made from
columns of twenty-five size 8/0 rocailles and one
dagger. The second skirt is made from columns of
one orange rocaille, five bugles (in different shades
of yellow and brown) and one black rocaille.

Materials

The beads are shown life-size to give a guide to the materials used whilst making the samples in this book (the threads are shown on page 26 & 27 of book one). It should be noted that the size of beads and their holes often vary, even in the same batch.

Rocaille or seed beads - Rounded glass beads that come in a range of finishes. They are available in different sizes: the higher the number, the smaller the bead.

Size 11/0   Size 8/0   Size 6/0

Pony beads - These are like large rocailles. They are available in glass or plastic.

Bugles - Long thin glass beads that come in a variety of finishes and sizes.

Double Delicas - Cylindrical beads with large, even holes.

Silver Rings - Doughnut shaped acrylic beads with a silver finish.

Silver Rounds - Spherical metal beads.

Findings - The general term for metal jewellery fittings that include: Bellcaps Clasps and Eyepins.

Materials

Faceted Beads - Many sided glass or plastic shapes. Available in many sizes, these are size 4mm.

Leaves - Glass beads shaped into leaves with a central hole at the top.

Daggers - Long tapered glass beads with a hole at the thinnest end.

Melons - One of a range of plastic shapes with large sized holes (approx. 5mm diameter)

Semiprecious Chips - beads made from misshapen pieces of semiprecious stones.

Lampwork beads - Individual beads hand-made by shaping glass over a hot flame.

Beading thread - A strong, fine thread that is often waxed. It is available from most bead suppliers and comes in a range of makes, sizes and colours.
Beading needles - fine needles with a long eye.

Suppliers

The thread suppliers remain the same as in book one, page 28. The beads used in this book were obtained from :

Spellbound Bead Company.
45, Tamworth Street, Lichfield,
Staffordshire, WS13 6JW.
Tel: 01543 417650

Stitch 'n' Craft (& Lynn Firth).
Swan's Yard, High Street,
Shaftesbury, Dorset, SP7 8JQ.
Tel: 01747 852500

London Bead Company.
339, Kentish Town Road,
London, NW5 2TJ.
Tel: 0870 2032323

GJ Beads.
Unit 1-3, Court Arcade, The Wharf,
St Ives, Cornwall, TR26 1LG.
Tel: 01736 793886

Bead Exclusive.
119-121, Teignmouth Road,
Torquay, Devon, TQ1 4HA.
Tel: 01803 322000

"Jazzy Lily Hot Glass".
Middle House, 34 Grecian Street,
Aylesbury, HP20 1LT.
Tel: 01296 437406

Diana East (& Glass Beadmakers UK)
19, King Street, Enderby,
Leicestershire, LE9 5NT.
Tel: 0116 2867664

Other useful addresses:

The Beadworkers Guild.
PO Box 24922
London, SE23 3WS

Peter Collingwood.
Blincoe's, Newlands Lane, Nayland,
Colchester, CO6 4JJ

For all other enquiries, including details of the Braid Society contact:

Carey Company.
Summercourt, Ridgeway,
Ottery St Mary
Devon, EX11 1DT
UK
Tel/fax: 01404 813486
E-mail: carey@careycompany.com
Website: www.careycompany.com